This symbol—three plumes of

steam rising from a pool of hot

water—indicates hot springs on

Japanese maps and is often

displayed at the entrance of

public baths and hot springs.

The Japanese phonetic

character yu *means "hot*

water" and is often displayed

at the entrance of public

baths.

How To Take A Japanese Bath

by Leonard Koren
illustrations by Suehiro Maruo

Stone Bridge Press
Berkeley, California

Thanks to Peter Goodman, Sam Kawakami, Taki
Ono, and Pamela Pasti for their invaluable help.
And special thanks to Elizabeth Freeman and Lyle
B. Mayer for their good-humored companionship
during the early days of gourmet bathing.

Art direction and design by the author.

Library of Congress Cataloging-in-Publication Data
Koren, Leonard.
    How to take a Japanese bath / by Leonard
    Koren : illustrations by Suehiro Maruo.
        p. cm.
ISBN 0-9628137-9-6 (trade paper)
ISBN 1-880656-00-0 (8-copy prepack)
    1. Bathing customs—Japan. I. Maruo,
    Suehiro. II. Title.
GT2846.J3K68   1992
391'.64—dc20   91-48055
                        CIP

Contents

Introduction

If there are but few things that can be called uniquely Japanese living culture, Japanese-style bathing is certainly one of them.

*

In Japan, clean and dirty are absolute and irreconcilable notions. Thus the Japanese logic of cleanliness dictates two parts to the bathing ritual: first washing and then soaking. Body washing involves soaping, scrubbing, and rinsing body dirt away. Soaking consists of doing nothing except sitting quietly and enjoying the moment.

*

The procedures outlined in this book apply to Japanese-style bathing anywhere in Japan: at home, at public baths, and at hot spring resorts.

1

Any time is a fine time to enjoy a
Japanese bath: on rising in the
morning, before retiring at night,
or whenever the inspiration
enters your mind.

2

Whether for bathing at home or at a public bathhouse, your bath kit should include: soap, shampoo, a washcloth, clean underwear and socks . . . and a plastic bucket for scooping water. The bucket doubles as a handy container for the other kit items, and is especially useful when strolling to the public bath.

3

To prepare the bath, first fill the
tub with hot water, testing it with
your hand to make sure it's the
right temperature for you. When
the tub is full, stir the water with
your hand or a stirring paddle to
blend the hot water on top with
the cooler water that tends
to sink to the bottom.

4

With the plastic bucket, scoop
some water from the tub and pour
it over your torso to rinse off
surface dirt. Continue scooping
and pouring, being sure to rinse
your private parts and anywhere
that it is especially grimy, like
your feet. Many people wash with
soap at this stage, but the choice
is yours. Just remember that the
cleaner you are, the cleaner the
water will be for the next
person who enters the bath.
Do be considerate.

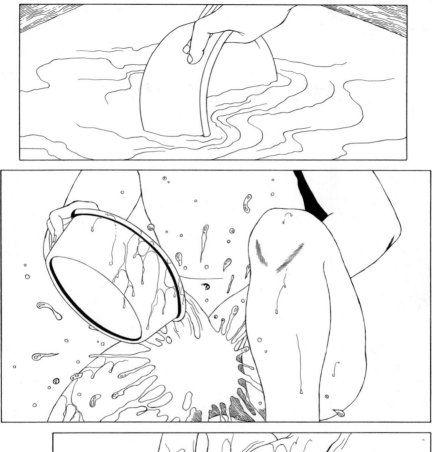

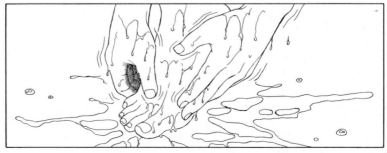

5

Gingerly, ease into the steaming
bath and sit quietly.

6

Soak until your body is
heated thoroughly, and then
get out carefully.

7

Using water from a wall faucet or
scooped from the tub, lather up
your washcloth with soap and
scrub yourself until you're
squeaky clean. This is also the
time to shampoo your hair if you
wish. Whatever you do, be careful
not to get any soap or suds
into the bath water.

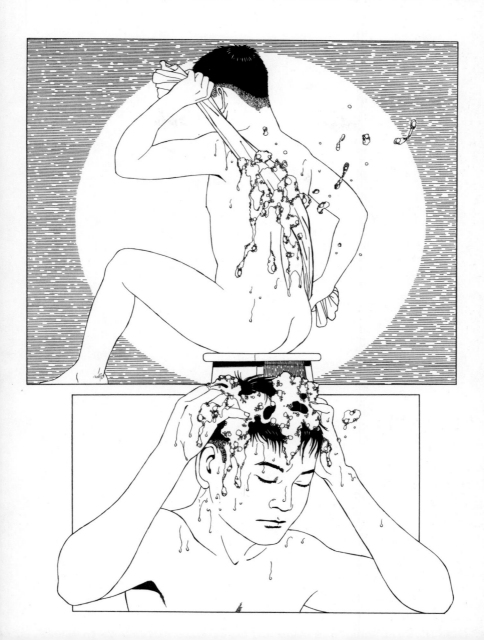

8

With fresh water from the tub or
wall faucet, thoroughly rinse
all the soap and shampoo
from your body.

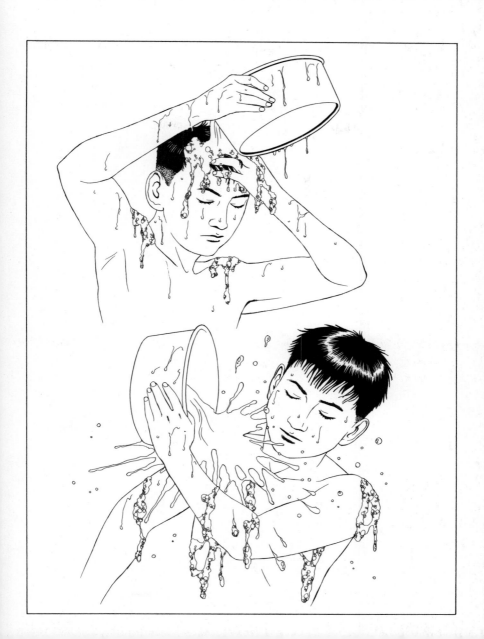

9

Ease back into the tub and enjoy a
good long soak. Feel your body
relax and any stress dissipate.
Pure bliss!

10

Bathing Japanese-style is often a communal activity where gentle conversation is an added pleasure. Sometimes you share a bath with your family. And sometimes, at a public bath or hot springs resort, you bathe with complete strangers. Public baths are usually divided into separate pools for men and women, but if you find yourself in a unisex bath, all you have to do is cover yourself modestly with your washcloth when walking around and otherwise bathe as usual.

11

As a courtesy to the next bather, skim any hair or debris off the surface of the water with a net when you are done. Then place the insulated cover on the tub to help keep the water hot. The next bather may add piping hot water to replace any that was scooped out or to increase the water temperature. Some Japanese bathtubs have built-in heaters that allow the water to be reheated while you soak or before the following day's bath. Many ecologically minded households recycle the bathwater after everyone in the family has bathed, using it for the first cycle in the washing machine, for watering the garden, and so on.

12

Après bath is a time for relaxing and cooling off. So find a comfortable spot where you can sit calmly and let magnificent thoughts fill your mind.

Overview

Bathing in Japan has always been more about getting pure than about getting clean. After all, the act of scrubbing the body free of dirt always takes place outside the tub. Only after the body is clean does the bather finally enter the water.

In ancient times—1,000 years ago—the "bath" was a natural hot pool, one of thousands created by Japan's proximity to a tectonic crash zone. Then the impurities exorcised by the bath were such things as death, disease, and menstrual blood. Today, the typical Japanese tub is a hollow of molded plastic and fiberglass, located indoors, and just big enough to sit in with your legs folded up to your chin. Still, the object is the same—not simply to rid yourself of the befoulment of the physical world but to cleanse the mind and spirit until the body is in tune with the forces of Nature. In the West, one works to avoid sin and to attain God's glory in the next life. In Japan, spiritual dirt is something that attaches to us all— like the reek of hair pomade or tobacco smoke—in the course of living, and can be easily removed by a daily bath.

Records shows that Buddhist temples in the 8th century maintained steam baths, sponsored in part by donations from wealthy nobles hoping to gain spiritual merit. The wealthy would personally assist in the bathing of the poor and sick, urged on by the example of the beautiful Empress Komyo. The empress was said to have a light emanating from her, indicating her high spiritual advancement. One day the light went out. She attributed this to her own lack of devotion and swore to bathe one thousand of the impoverished and infirm of all ages and sexes. The last person who came to her was a leper—or perhaps the Buddha disguised as a leper. But the empress did not hesitate, and upon bathing him immediately her aura returned.

The first commercial public bath—or *sento*—was built in the 1590s, and entrepreneurs throughout the country soon were opening up their own bathhouses. Food, conversation, games, and sexual pleasures became a part of the bath scene. Water replaced steam. In the late 19th century the government banned mixed-sex bathing. But the *sento* remained the equivalent of the medieval European well—the place where the community gathered to see and be seen, to exchange news and gossip.

With the construction of modern housing, the *sento* is disappearing at a rapid rate from urban Japan. But over 12,000 still exist. Many have attached laundromats, so that your clothes can soak at the same time you do. Public baths are generally open from four in the afternoon until midnight. In their egalitarian atmosphere you can get warm, chat with your neighbors (many of whom have baths at home but come to enjoy the *sento* anyway), and enjoy a generous volume of architectural space. Often there is a striking mural of a street scene or landscape on the back wall that you can lose yourself in as you sink into the tub.

Almost every *sento* adheres to the same basic plan: At the entrance you remove your shoes. Then you walk beyond a curtain or sliding door to the men's or women's side, where you pay the attendant the equivalent of about two dollars. Then you undress and, with your bath kit (shampoo, washcloth, etc.), move on to the washing and soaking area.

A more naturalistic version of the *sento* can be found at any of the thousands of hot springs (*onsen*) throughout the Japanese countryside. The bathing environment here usually includes a sensitive use of wood, stone, and other natural elements such as ferns and waterfalls. *Onsen* baths usually have men's and women's sections, but the farther you go from the big cities, the less important are divisions by gender. When the baths are actually outdoors (*rotenburo*) there is often no separation between the sexes at all. Here, a deft use of the *tenugui*, an elongated cotton washcloth, provides as much modesty as is required. (After the bath, this same washcloth is used as a drying towel— wrung out and used over and over again like a sponge on the body.)

The home bath is an altogether different experience, since it is solitary and confined. Perhaps it is a metaphor for the nuclearization of the Japanese family, and as such its ascendancy may have dire consequences for the traditional culture. Drawing a full bath every day when a shower would do, particularly if you're living alone, is what the Japanese call *mendokusai*: a bother.

But the old ways die hard, and this is immediately noticeable even in the most modern Japanese apartment: the vulgar toilet is almost always in a different compartment from where the body is bathed and purified. The bath in Japan remains that special place where the mind is cleansed as the body steeps in its own physicality.

NOTE: The Japanese word for bath is *furo*. Water is kept very hot in most Japanese baths, much hotter than in the conventional American hot tub. If you are pregnant, older, or have any serious medical—particularly heart- or **circulation-related—problems, check with** a physician about the advisability of Japanese-style bathing. ALSO: Although Japanese revelers sometimes consume alcoholic beverages prior to bathing, particularly at *onsen* inns, this is not recommended.

This symbol—three plumes of

steam rising from a pool of hot

water—indicates hot springs on

Japanese maps and is often

displayed at the entrance of

public baths and hot springs.

The Japanese phonetic character yu *means "hot water" and is often displayed at the entrance of public baths.*